Eros Proposes a Toast

Eros Proposes a Toast

Collected Public Poems and Gifts

Tony Conran

seren

seren is the book imprint of
Poetry Wales Press Ltd
Wyndham Street, Bridgend, Wales

© Tony Conran 1998
The moral right of Tony Conran to be identified
as the author of this work has been asserted

ISBN 1-85411-235-X

A CIP record for this title is available from the British Library

Cover design: Simon Hicks

The publisher acknowledges the financial support of the
Arts Council of Wales

Printed in Plantin
by The Cromwell Press Ltd, Trowbridge

Contents

Blodeuwedd and Other Poems

New Poems

Formal Poems

For Dylan Thomas

Poor poetry is gone to seed:
Footnotes in damp verse must plead
The rigour of her proper creed
      In their excuse,
While prosemen with her direst need
      Play fast and loose.

But you, sir, made with abstract art
Appropriate mansion for the heart,
A territory kept apart
      Cunning with phrases
Woven as unicorn and hart
      In lovelit mazes.

Fired with the wheeling stanza, caught
Between the image and the thought,
In a wasteland of flurry and doubt
      You'd stand the hurtle,
Warrior of tenses, undistraught
      By Christ or mortal.

By womblight through the dreamdank ways,
Don Quixote of the vaunted phrase,
Under our viaduct of days
      You'd dare to wander
In youth and innocence of praise
      To wield God's thunder.

Where love's apocalypse unrolled
The sorrowing sperm that, blind and bald,
Decides our fortune in the cold
      Outwombward travel,
You were entangled by the old
      Gift of gab devil.

Redeemed by grief, your falcon flashed
Into its native light at last:
Ann's bard, you stood forth unabashed
      In childlike glory:
Sculptor of change, the secret past
      Stole into story.

Childhood was yours, and devil may care,
Heron and gallows hawk and hare,
Priest of the chapeldownunder air
And steepled town,
Before the heart was still, my dear,
Or bone lay down.

1954

For the Marriage of Heulwen Evans

As wind, as trees in tumult, haphazard
   As rocks in Nant Ffrancon,
  As the sea dusted with dawn,
  I'd deal for you my blessing.

May love be gentle as a moth, stroking
   The moon upon rushes;
  Like a lark into sunlight
  May he go glad to your bed.

Generous may he be, and strong, like a lord
   Conniving no mischief;
  Honourable in the world,
  And to you, always splendid!

Tall in Llyn Ogwen reflected hills
Are by the ripples shut in black bars:
So I, no matter how I turn, always
  My hope is waived, and no true image.

But of your children may be made whole
All fragmentary generations,
And the calm lake of your Welsh truth body
  The ancient mountains, rock for hard rock.

           1956

Elegiac Ode for R. Williams Parry

(Welsh Poet, d. 1955)

A'm gwlad gynnevin
Yw bro ser hevin
   – The Book of Taliesin

(And my original country is
the region of summer stars)

Dead poet, behind time hidden, through two wars
       Two mockeries of peace
     And two betrayals, you fought
     The beast-black nails of preachers,

Did battle against roarers, and at night
       Came to the spring waters,
     Cantered between fresh birches
     To the cold moon in a pond.

And your wounds awoke in the night air, shone
       In the wind like fireflies,
     And in the chill ditch were healed,
     In the blear weed and stillness.

The wood is ancient, though leaf's young,
And the frog sings such old motets
     To ease his stomach
     And his old tup's lust
     That none remember
       First time he croaked!

Yet the pond with its shattered moon
Rots to such diluvian vintage
     Not even the frog
     For all his gossip
     Can put genesis
       To these waters.

The inmost covert of five trees
In the deep wood in the hollows
		Tucked in the foothills
		In the secret part
		Of the difficult land
			Of all poets

Is where we'd seek you, your music
Having entranced our weak daydreams
		And your wounds glinting
		Like frosty rivers
		That we always knew
			Ran through our land.

(For his love it was, we'd argue,
This wistful, antiquated wood
		Where all visions end
		And the hurt stabs out
		No more with vivid
			And desperate drums.)

But having come there, no small hardship
Considering our stature, over hill
And blitzed escarpment, our donkeys, half blind
		With flies, plodding where you were speedy,

Down to the cold woods of the goblin
And the orange-green moon, and to ditch
Where all your starry wounds were sweet, and so
		To the five trees and the pondfast frog,

And having come there, our enquiries
After your ghost: has he returned yet?
Were but met by a giggling owl, and the frog's
		Lugubrious chant: not here! not here!

No, he'll not come, though, in his day, he loved
    This tree-shadowed cauldron.
That dark original country
Where he visits, has no knife
To peel his heart, neither hemlock
Nor nail, but only the singing,
The tuned begetting of bards, the brazen
    Ecstasy in darkness.

How could wounds, in that bed of planets, shine
    Out-heroding glow-worms?
When you had shrunk to a shaving
Of grey flesh, cold in the churchyard,
And december mourners hurried
To the hereafters of homage,
We mistook utterly your end, trusting
    To a ditch of moonshine.

Wherever in the yellow bones
Of speaking, phrase turns its fingers
    To touch our bodies,
    Your immanent ghost
   Walks proudly in bright eyes.

Whether a gipsy begs water;
Whether old quarrymen debate
    By ramshackle bus
    Football or bible
  Or grumble about cold;

Whether the new teacher forgets
His children no longer listen;
    Whether ovation
    Ends the charm or no,
  Or the bard goes hungry –

In all gay words, in all complaints,
Blasphemies or valedictions,
    The eyes tell their tale,
    Poet, whose homeland
  Harks to the summer stars!

And we can meet him, almost see him
For that moment between experience
And recognition, and hear, soft and cold
    His shepherd voice in gravel glinting.

Where the hill wind is free, attentive
To the tongues of chiffchaff and curlew,
His meditating feet walk still, private
    As stoat down the dingles of gorse.

His old eyes that for their betterment
Wished he was deaf once, down to the cwm
Hurry like bumblebees, anxious to tell
    The exact marking and fashion of rocks.

How should that surprising awe go down
Without himself that gave it utterance?
And for the dead, being dead, how should words
    Of his / sorrow for mortal kindness?

We'll find him, like his own fox, between
Dry-stone walls not far from the village;
With one foot hesitant, eyes flaming – he's there
    And again, sudden as a star, is gone!

1956

Poems 1951-67

Instead of a Gift

for Julie Dwyer

All day, I have tried to carve for you a shrine
From old lengths of applewood, stubs of hard oak,
Various timber ends, cherry and sweet-scented pine
That came I cannot remember how or where –
Lebanon maybe, or sprouting with wild olive
Above Corinth, or the Arkadian hills: mostly
From English woods, and a few from Wales.

I imaged a crib; a coronation of Mary the virgin;
Three crosses then, a Christopher, a preaching Francis
With his brother the thrush: scene after scene.
I smiled as each was firmed into my shrine
That I would give you, soon as glue was set,
Plump haloes lit with gold, and my craftsman's hand
That had not lost its cunning, satisfied at last.

Luck was against me: as each heartfelt icon
Grew to my chisel, some careless lunge,
Failure of nerve or quirk of bad perspective
Bungled the job. I threw the lame wood aside.
Timber that had embarrassed me before
To choose good pieces, now was scarce and small.
With fretsaw fragments, I would twist and fine
To a pattern-work simpler, not so wasteful...

In vain. The devil of this timber has not consented,
Broke delicate spars, chipped features over-subtle,
Bleared my eye. At last, I'd only this tiny block,
Applewood, love's tree, timber of doubtful choices.
My knife hardly has courage to carve.
I scratch my name and yours above a tree
With twenty golden apples, as you have years
This nineteenth of November, and as many choices
Delicate as Eve's, to come before old age.

It is hardly a shrine, this crude and scrawled on wood
With its tree and two names. But let it pass
For what it is, a talisman for choices.
Possess it, make it yours. Have it to die with you.

1961

Success

Well, I am glad and say, Let public virtues
And private loves with oak and wild roses
Be crowned, and the broad palm be cut.

Your happiness is mine. The dance moves on,
The sifting light for a moment
Crowns you with golden hopes.

These certain things
Give you Good-health by day
And happy nights!

1962

The Bombing of Guernica

A Recitation to Music
for Bernard Rands

Guernica was bombed by German aircraft on 26th April, 1937. It was the first undefended town to be blitzed from the air, the prototype of Coventry, Dresden and Hiroshima. Guernica, the Basque capital, was bombed on Monday, the market day, so the town was full. First the streets were machine-gunned, then bombed with high explosives, then with incendiaries. This pattern was repeated till dusk.

Dark labourers pondered this April day
the black enrobement of fat wives.

Still life of an early morning. Harsh shadow and hard light.
Tenderness and brutality in the gesture of laying a cup.

Barn life. Yard life. Devotional
chickens peck and squawk in the muck.

Old fury to old fury
Rumours with jeering malice
What their own Swastika shall do.

(Swastika, hope of the world,
Whose eyes bulge through thick spectacles
To a yawning sun ...)

Hag unto hag reports
This mourning that shall come to market
Like a farmer.

The black birds stand in the corners of the sky.
Their talons are bright,
Their eyes dull with the mechanical
Violence of street louts.

The black birds are ultimate cynics. Sunlight
Is pretext to be dead,
To be herded into death like cattle,
To kill with the brilliant gold of bullets.

They lift their talons to the sky, these black birds,
And delicately tilt their wings
To a precision of narrow prey.
They pockmark the cobbles with gold.

The sky is ripe and yellow like an apple.
The sea questions the horizon, the blue drum
Of the Atlantic is felt amid lemons.
The bloodshed of countless sunsets
Has come to roost in the town of yellow walls.

A bride in the churchdoor in her white veil
Has smiled to the golden suitor. Old women
At solemn vespers of their toothless gossip
Scutter profanely to shelter in screech and nudeness
Pain's undiscriminating phallus of gold.

The bloodshed of many an Atlantic sunset
Ricochets from children. Priest carries Calvary
And dies of a blind man's spear in the kidney
And is crossed as he dives to a nameless death
In the panic of a calling far beyond his.

And the proud birds that stand in the sky's corners
Look uncomplainingly down at the saffron city
With its public emptiness emphatic with corpses,
Its wailing masked by their engines, its mourning
Phlegmatic to their height as starving beggars.

The yellow walls still stand in the applelight
Of an afternoon immemorially transparent
And the gold blood on the cobbles
Is inviting as a widow. Swastika's drum
Must be Pied Piper, call rats from quaking holes.

The black birds gather, then with a scream
Target the saffron town. Façades crumble.
Swastika's great drum echoes along blue gorges
To drag the huddling mobs from privacy
Under the talons wailing for dead man.

Blossoming mornings of winter,
Put no face to the child that sleeps.

Put no feature, no eye or lip,
To the body that sleeps in frost.

Don't remember the sickness of touching
That smouldering charred face

Or the tomb we founded for God
On bones of vomiting gold.

Strict acid light of morning,
Put no face to the child that sleeps.

1962

Voyage from Cythera

– a rejoinder to John Danby when he said he was tired of 'the young in one another's arms,' and like Yeats wanted to 'sail the seas and come / to the holy city of Byzantium.' Cythera is the island of Venus in Watteau's painting, L'embarquement pour l'île de Cythère.

Rain mists the glass, the summer-flinging wind
Bottom-gears hikers, calmed to a groan
In huddled pubs, clouded with anoraks.
Lovers have set out marching into hills,
Pillioned on bikes along black roads,
Or two by two come to the dinghy'd port
To tack like double stars, conjoint in locking wind –
One leans with wet hair and smarting palms
Out over tiderace, the other trims their course.
And all the dissolute joy is jammed by the rain.

Where does a man sail out *from* Cythera?
Political passions erode on further coasts.
All tugs towards freedom. Mood-wearied men,
Gaunt under mulct of generation's curse,
Saunter at dawn down to rusted wharves
To listen and be tempted, where the bellbuoys
At harbour mouth direct embarking sailors
To leave their fancy bints, their wives
At cottage doors, and drowsy daughters,
Seeking the werewolf mother of the floods –
That fiend enchantress! Memory, memory...
Erosion of politics, ten years at Troy,
Vasco da Gama, after Phoenician oars.

The Greeks thought memory the Muse's mother
Who orders times to a twinkle of words
Like foam through pebbles. Zeus was her father –
I imagine him, the archaic god
Older than turtles, Silenus-like,
With a light step and a walking stick,
Jauntily All-Present, Adsum of himself.
I imagine him, in fact, rather like you.

Is that why, sir, Byzantium's clockwork
Seems little excuse to exit from this Island?
Be father to the mothers of my songs.
The rain and the wind clamour of other journeys –
But has the Storm daughters? Growing things
Require old gods to make green memories fertile.

1963

Elegy for Sir Ifor Williams

scholar and editor

Does a word as a widow in the brain
    On the broad page of woe
    Make outcry, sigh for him so
    To sere an old heart's sorrow?

At a loss is Taliesin, the Black Book
    Is bleak, and Aneirin;
    On a bed where learning's been
    The ravens take their ravin.

    Sea-eagles feed at midday;
    Too soon they peck at sinew;
    Kite, crow and hawk make outcry;
    Claws upon red flesh they cloy.

Where is Cynddylan's ransom, or Heledd's
    To make hale his wisdom?
    As deep as the tongue is dumb
    The drab dust keeps his custom.

At Catraeth troops took outrage; with the dawn
    They died for the mead wage:
    The quarrier of their courage
    Lies raw to the Slayer's rage.

Three hundred, dead in a day, into war
    Went warriors on foray:
    We mind upon this Monday
    What he was is locked away.

1965

Translating Welsh Poetry

Bedwyr, the frantic burden
Wholly cuts me off from men.
It's what makes me not notice
The too much time that I miss.
So hard – the hazard is huge
I deal against a deluge
While a dotty world yet wags
Trumps from a thousand handbags.
Tomorrow and tomorrow –
Each day's a leech, lays me low.
So hard, to string in English
The tied Welsh that I would wish
And scan without cynghanedd,
Heart's clamour, labour of lathe,
Hammer-stroke – how I'm stricken! –
To give, I'm at it again,
A mirror of its merit
To the cywydd wild with wit.

1965

To John Wain

The run to Rhosgadfan
    In gossip-geared buses,
A scherzo in snatches
    Round hedgerow and rushes –

A world in your wildtrack,
    John Wain, you have waiting:
In rhyme or regaling
    You've style to your shaping.

Past pylon and postbox,
    Three louts, an old woman –
Nos da, rwan, then sudden
    Ta-ra to Rhostryfan.

And there's your white cottage –
    Good quits for a million,
A banco of bullion
    For Ianto and William.

How many take refuge
    In rare Llwyn Eilian,
The high heart in welcome,
    The sharp eye of Eirian.

Sweet mist of the mountain –
    Next stop, call to cabman!
I'm young as old Adam
    This run to Rhosgadfan.

1965

CLAIM CLAIM CLAIM

Claim

An Insurance Cantata

The casualty experience for 1966 continued to deteriorate, the total losses recorded being about 20% higher than those in 1965. A partial recovery had occurred by the end of the year at which time, however, the United States Dow Jones Index had fallen by 19%. Against this background it is not unsatisfactory that the depreciation in the Life Fund was less than 6% overall. Apart from the high incidence of claims, 1966 was in many respects a difficult year. Nevertheless we can look back with satisfaction on the progress made towards complete integration within.

Brotikuk kuk brotik brotik
kukit kukit brotik
kuk kubrokit kubrot
kubrot kubrot kuk kubrot

CLAIM   CLAIM   CLAIM

against tackle
against gear
against belt
against wheel

against bullet
against bomb
against gas
against gun

Claim of the women turning up fortunes,
Agnostic horoscopes on cornered pages,
Claim of the stars, by the right of the Zodiac,
By the birthright of a sign, Aquarius, Gemini,
The Ram, the Crab, the weighted Scales

Kuk kubrokit kubrot

Claim of the wasting strength of a man
Rivalry at once both anxious and even

Brotikuk kubrot kubrot

Claim of the dreams that terrify small children
Claim of the good grass and the unbroken light
Claim of the nudging shadow of alders

        where the kingfisher flies
                       swift and blue
        startles, yet does not surprise
        or break
               the rigour of the waiting gloom

Kuk kuk kuk

Claim of the toy sword against the real
The fury of play against the play of our fury

Kuk kubrokit kubrot

Kuk kubrokit kubrot

CLAIM   CLAIM   CLAIM

        against the slovenly nursemaids of danger
        against the practitioners of plague
        against the apostolic addicts of poison
        against the bored surgeons of the germ

Kukit kukit brotik
Kuk kubrokit kubrot

        against the gatherer of fruit that denies the fruit
        against the hunter that does not kill his friend
        against the farmer that denies the cock and the bull
        the man that denies the child

Kuk kubrokit kubrot

        against the anaesthetists of anger
        against the consultants that do not speak

Brotikuk kuk brotik brotik
kukit kukit brotik
kuk kubrokit kubrot
kuk kuk kuk

Kuk kuk kuk

Claim of the mortal man in the midmost of his way
In the light years of heaven a fathom of darkness

Claim of the girlhood and boyhood of things
In the breakdown of stars, to be awkward and rich

Claim of the angel to realise the brute
Claim of the living to death, of the dying to live

CLAIM   CLAIM   CLAIM

A Toast to John Wain

on his poem 'Ferns, for Anthony Conran in Bangor' from *Letters to Five Artists*

England is far from me. But you,
John, in whom England still breeds true,
    Rouse me from my Welsh sleep
    Where, perching on the steep

I winter in deciduous brown
Above a damp and fungoid town.
    I hear you speak of me
    Between stone and grey sea

And hear your generous rash praise
Wind in with channel-curdled phrase
    In a high tide of art
    Over my pebbly heart.

It is no small thing – no small grace –
To be addressed, in such a place,
    By such a man as you,
    John, and with fondness too,

As poet, bringer of peace and friend.
Is there, humanly, a higher end?
    My cup's full to the brim,
    My ears ring, my eyes swim,

About my 'Ferns' I look and look ...
And first, for you and for your book
    I'm happy, pouring out
    Libations all about

To that patronal Ovidian ghost
You pledged the first. And then I toast
    The rest of us, the five
    Artists chosen and alive

And lastly, you that chose – our part
In the exchequer of your art
    The currency of us all
    Till English and England fall!

1969

Dial-a-Poem

Hello. Poem speaking. POEM. Yes P-O-E-M, Poem. That's
    what you wanted, wasn't it, what you ordered, wasn't
    it, what the slot in the telephone booth said you could
    have?

A genie for a genius, a poem, a poem, a poem –
    to reassure you, to console you, to put you in touch,
    to touch you, to touch, to encapsulate the world,
    to bring you a whiff of beauty from old Wales
    (wasn't it?) to trouble you – gently – like the smell
            of worn leather,
    to tell you truths which lie too deep for tears?

Well, this is it. Are you standing comfortably?
    Are you standing at ease?
    Are you silent upon a peak in Darien?

Then I'll begin.

I'll begin at the beginning. God save the Queen. GOD SAVE
    THE QUEEN. By whose five new pennies, neatly indented
    like Veronica's hankie with her own spitting and perspiring
    likeness, the five wounds, the five sorrowful mysteries of
    Wales on the walk to the Paradise Garden, by the five new
    pennies of the Queen –

I am called, I am invoked, I am conjured out of two bits of
    wire and the ingenuity of mortal invention to OBEY YOU,
    anonymously ringing my eternal tinkler at the other end –
    the very far nowhere end –

my dear master, my cheaply anonymous master, with your five
    moonshine pennies minted by the grace of Empire in Wales,
    in Wales, in the land of the eponymous fathers, by the
    Queen's hands unemployed in Glamorgan –

I'll begin at the beginning. A deep depression over Caernarfon
    is veering east. A trough of low pressure from the derelict
    pseudo-shires of Montgomery and Merioneth, caught in the
    broker-trades and the fifteen-plus, is

causing rot along the frontiers of reasonable expectations. Visibility will be as far as your nose will take you. South-east cones have been hoisted on the coaltips of Morgannwg and Gwent. There may be some sunlight over hired ground.

We are dying, Egypt, dying. By the red sea, by the dead sea, by the waters of Babel, by the waters of Efyrnwy and Tryweryn, by the tidal possibilities latent in crude oil and natural gas, by the tolling of motorcars over the bridges, by the rain, by the snow, by the depressional oblivion of Merthyr and Tonypandy –

I'll begin at the beginning. That was THE WEATHER. That was LIFT UP YOUR HEARTS. That was BOOK AT BEDTIME. That was THE EPILOGUE. God save the Queen.

Here is the Zero-hour news. The World at Zero. Here is the News. Are you standing comfortably?

Then I'll begin.

1969

Gifts

(from *Spirit Level*)

Bay Leaves

for Richard B. White

Brittle, matt-surfaced,
Lanceolate
With the points tipped like spears,
The edges undulate –

Their dark green elegance
Modestly proper for us
Retainers of the Muse,
And dangerous –

Sweet-scented, like old age,
Arrowheads
Tipped with the embalmer's spice
Of the undead –

These leaves from my hedge
Unshrivelled yet
In this mild January –
These leaves pay my debt,

Poet, for your excitement
And lust for the word's skin
Rippling over the breath
At the drop of a pin.

1969

To Ask for a Bugle

from Euros Bowen, prifardd *

A thick tapering trumpet,
A rhizome of bronze
In a dark forge moulded and twisted
In spiralling rounds.

A wide bloom opens from the root –
A crater of red
Like a lake of smouldering molten stone
Erupts from its bed –

At the thin snakelike mouthpiece
An oracle of death
Through the pursed lips, teeth, tongue,
Straitens its breath.

You know the horn I speak of,
Whose formal cry
Gives ecstasy; whose hot bray
Commands men die.

1969

* Prifardd, lit. chief poet, but used now of poets who have been chaired or crowned at an eisteddfod

Toy Chariot

for Vikki, when I took her to see Victor Neep the artist, his wife Phyllis, and
his children Paul, who played classical guitar, and Katie, who was reading a
teenage magazine

From the keys of three beer-cans
Vic's fingers worked
This sculptured toy wagon
As we played and talked.

A tin chariot, a moon car
For a Pegasus
No higher than your thumb
He made for us.

Parked on the edge of memories –
Talk, beer, guitars,
A white room charred with paintings
Proud of its scars...

Live your life, do your thing –
Paul's pharaoh stance
In the pyramids of Bach;
Katie's neat glance

At the extravagance of her elders;
Vic being Vic
In the ferocity of his kindness
And compassionate wit;

Your own haunted eyes
Wild as a bird
Trapped between the generations
Like an old slang word;

And I, your persecutor,
Walking so still
Where the trap of my love had sprung
Against my will.

You have torn away since
Like a young fox
To your natural hill country
Where lichened rocks

Camouflage you panting
In the red fern
Till the blood scabs, the wound heals,
Quickness returns.

Did your terrified struggling teeth
Put this hurt
On my hands, bedraggle with red
The sleeve of my shirt?

I have broken the trap's spring.
I am hungry and cold.
A landscape of miles of silence
Begins to unfold.

What I could give you, I cannot;
What you gave me
Is lost in the acid acres
Of peat and scree.

Here is Vic's toy. It is yours,
I resign my part.
When you need to know what you are,
Conjure this cart

– Emblem of trusting each other
In the alone –
Winged Pegasus between the shafts,
Hoof hard on stone,

Parked on the curb of memories,
Speech, beer, song –
A moon car, a tin chariot
Two lifetimes long.

1969

Spirit Level

for George and Sue, in New Guinea

An odd gift, certainly. One
Would have to be hard up
To give such a thing for a wedding.
A plate or a cup

Of Eighteenth Century pot –
Rustic, of course,
Embellished with two seated lovers
And a grazing horse;

Or else a spied treasure of bronze
From Samarkand –
A perfectionist's quodlibet
From a shop on the Strand –

Ah, these would be elegant gifts
And surely would raise
The naked Papuans to envy
The White Man's ways.

I wish I had thought of them sooner
Or luck had slunk
To the wellnigh miraculous gift
In a shopful of junk.

But my eye has domiciled with this
Uncompromising wood,
Its brass fittings inelegant,
Its proportions crude.

Drab product of a technology
That has left it behind,
A tool mass-produced without passion
Of body or mind...

But through its window the small, oblong
Bubble of oil
– Wherever you are, on English
Or New Guinean soil –

Still keeps its strange relationship
To the round earth
And points to the perfect tangent
Of its spheroid girth.

The awe-inspiring simplicity
Of that design
Makes irrelevant lack of grace
And brutal line.

Such is my emblem for how I honour you,
For what I give
Comes from the responding eye
Where all truths live.

I pray for you through this emblem
That each of you in each,
The straight wood, the bubble of oil,
True centre reach,

And right-angled with the world,
Hold its full sphere
With the delicate poise
Of the hoof of a deer.

1969

Three Lily Seeds

for a birthday

Beata immaculati in via – Psalm 118

The trumpets blow for me. They haunt
My green vision
Like an army marching, or an angelic
Visitation.

Leaves heavy along the woods
Suddenly take flight
As the flame and passion of falling
Blows them light

Twittering down, heaping in ochre
Yellow and red
To the soft dust and brown velvet
Of the roots' wide bed.

Here, last November, I excavated
Three holes in the mould
For these monocot lordlings to winter
Their ivory and gold.

Bulbs dark as well-handled leather,
Fragile shoots
Of easily broken green tissue
And bruisable roots.

Now, nearly November again, I look back
On those days in June
Where the primitive leaf-ringed stem, like a sapling,
Climbed into bloom.

The trumpets blow for me. The gold stamens
Lick at white flesh
With its womb at the green hub secret
In the veins mesh.

Pagodas reach treeward. I walk
The chiming ground
Where the three lilies' Buddha-nature
Rings round me like sound.

I pluck from them one brown fruit, a double pod
Beginning to split,
And shake out into my palm
Three seeds from it –

Three flat irregular polygons, like fragments
Of a Dead Sea scroll,
Each with its scripturing embryo
Torn from the whole.

We live in an age of grass –
Fine lines, quick returns.
The drama of the Prairies
Our attention earns.

The savannah and the wheatfield
Have made us Man.
The grasses shaped us to their ends
As only grass can.

What lily has made us labour all day
Up to our knees
In a paddy-field full of wet mud
Like the Chinese?

The shepherd leads his flock to pasture –
Lilies don't suit
Even to shape his oaten pipe
Or bamboo flute!

No cities are born from the lily-fields.
A surplus of seed
Less elaborately blue-blooded by half
Answers our need.

All flesh is grass. The grasses are masters.
Regard with awe
That bit of grey-with-rain lawn
At the street door:

Our most poised technological delicacy
Is but crude
To the Ockham's razor implicit in a grass-flower's
Omni-aptitude.

Lilies indeed! Had it been left to the *Liliaceae*
We'd still swing from trees
Fruit-guzzlers contented with jungle
Like chimpanzees.

And yet... and yet... I walk
On the chiming ground
Where the three lilies' Buddha-nature
Sounds through me and round.

And it is lily-seeds, Barbara, I give you
And not an ear
Of wheat or a cob of maize
For your twentieth year.

1969

Fern Frond

for John Wain

Why don't I send you
A fern really old –
Osmunda, with its massive
Stump-like bole?

Marattia or *Angiopteris* –
Squat little trees
That through the millenia
Inched down by degrees –

Dowagers of the rain forests
Left to their plight
In the hundred yard high
Struggle for light –

Or *Lygodium*, the last
Climbing fern –
Queens that hark back to a realm
Of no return?

No, the Ghost Dance is over.
Redskin encampment
Knows no more dreams. Paleface
Magic's too rampant.

Not even suicide, not even
A fight to the death.
Only the necessity
Not to waste breath.

Only the immutable gene
Sullen beyond fear,
Only the getting drunk
On white man's beer.

No, John, this is a frond
Quite other than those
That were ousted by a flower
From Eden groves.

Evolved, sophisticated,
Able to hold
Its own where it chooses to be,
Withstanding the cold

Of our British winters
Like birch or oak.
Red leaf burns on the hill.
Red dreams turn to smoke.

This fern has no royal blood –
Or if it has
Only as much as is green
In a blade of grass.

Long after the Battle of the Trees
Was lost, and flowers
And fruits began to flaunt
Imperial powers,

Creating for their use
Insect, beast and bird,
Learning the way of quick returns –
Decay and rebirth:

Long after that, in an Atlantis
Buried under the snows –
A lost Antarctic world
Before the ice floes

Clanged to about it, and all
That was left
Of the whole teeming continent
Was blizzard and drift:

In that Reservation of quiet
The ferns gathered,
Changed, held their ground, and evolved.
Flowers weren't bothered.

Earth heaves over again.
Land masses clash
And rebound from each other.
Continents mash.

New sporelings wander the world –
Perch high in the trees,
Clothe banks, and float in the streams,
Colonize screes.

And Bracken rakes in his gold,
A great tycoon,
A subterranean emperor
Every June

Uncurling his gloved firsts
Even against Grass –
A bit nouveau riche,
Just a bit brash!

But the Dryopterids (one of whose
Young fronds this is)
Keep the Fern's Way perhaps clearer
Than all of these.

They grow in the shade of woods,
By streams or rocks,
Tough-fronded, fibrous-rooting,
With short blunt stocks.

They have lost the extravagant zest
Of the ancient trees.
You can't collect sackfuls of spores
Whenever you please.

They are modest things, friendly
In a fashion
And without great animosity
Or competitive passion.

John, don't be misled. They aren't *us*.
Tolerance is cheap.
They've no love for the animal kingdom.
They murder sheep.

They go out of their way to be useless.
They wear long hair.
They smoke hash in quakerish meetings.
They DO NOT CARE.

There's no hope in a fern, not a bit.
They've detachable sex.
Their spores are dehydrated lust –
Add water, and mix.

1970

Silver Spoon

for Cynan, my godson

Light in the half-inch bowl
Reflected
Is a star blazing in an argent field,
The shield trisected

Where it lies, by a corner of walls and ceiling
White and gold,
Filled with the radiant grain of metal
Myriadfold.

The slender stem reaches upward
Like a flower stalk
To the crest where a squat little dragon
Ungainly walks.

I'm a bit nonplussed about giving you
Such a trinket.
It won't keep you warm. It won't love you.
You can't eat or drink it.

But today, like one of the Kings,
I come from far.
Little World-Saviour, I fulfil your rites,
I follow your star.

They will pour the water over your face,
My holy one,
And yourself not sure yet whether birth was good
Or wisely done.

They will fold great hands about you. Waters
Will wet your eyes.
The cold rain darkens on the rocks of your exile,
Falls from blind skies.

Child, it is difficult. Having got used to the dry
Feel of world, yet
To be pressured again, and shocked into birth's
Strenuous wet.

Nor can gifts help. They hardly make sense:
How can I give
When the concept GIFT is not separable
From how you live?

How futile my timely present
Becomes in this Now
Where the christening waters of Bethlehem
Crown your brow!

Yet what I have brought, I must give.
I could not stand
In this spot where all is offered
With a void in my hand.

Gifts whose only point is the formal
Act of giving
Can arbitrarily be given meaning
Like charms for living.

All I can give are symbols
Of once and soon –
Heraldic things – gold, frankincense, myrrh –
A silver spoon.

When you are four or five, they will hand it you,
Cynan, and say:
'Your godfather gave you this
On your christening day.'

And you will look at the little Welsh dragon
And see the shield
Where the light's trapped like a blazing star
In an argent field.

It will remind you where you were born,
And perhaps you'll guess
How a wise man seeing your star in the east
Came to bless.

1970

Heron

for the Wedding of Brian and Margaret

Sword gleam, perpendicular Gothic grotesque
And a long stoop
Of saint's patience, an ancient King's Messenger's
Elegant droop –

And yet not entirely antique:
Quick as a wish
The radar-true lunge of its beak,
Sniper of fish –

No, I was not mistaken!
In the nature of things
In that reedbed, coasting from mud to mud
Those square-rigged wings

Hardly glimpsed, could only have meant
His eminence
Was abroad and stalking
The bank's long distance...

Yes, there he goes! Never can I find a heron
Without it being
A love gift and a revelation
Of the power of all seeing.

For five seconds or so, I can stare
With my eyes clean
Of the entanglement of *should be*
Or *ought to have been.*

I did not imagine it. It is there.
I become the bird.
My sight moves over the waters.
I AM, the Word.

For the blind eye reaches to vision
And in love alone
Natura naturans
Knows and is known.

O but love must hurry, must hurry,
Weigh up odds and plan
Natura naturata
In the scheme of Man –

A stitch in time, a kiss,
The tactics of food,
The memory's conserving
Of all that is good...

A marriage is for home –
We know it, and vow
That Nature be be-natured
In this home, now.

And yet, this poem of mine
Made for you
On the day that you vouched for a home
That is kind and true,

Concerns no home at all
But a wild fen
And a heron coasting from mud to mud
Through driving rain.

1970

Silver

for Jill on her birthday

A galeful of rain explodes
Like fireworks
Over the black street
In a spray of sparks.

Into a detonation of silver
I dance, I fly.
It singes my hair. My coat tails
Flap down the sky.

It is strange how you
– So gold, so warm –
In November of all months
Contrived to be born!

Silver of twenty-five years
Glints on the dark
Debris of thought
Like exploding sparks.

Silver, the moon metal,
Whose salts are white
And alive in the darkness,
Blacken with light.

Silver, the inward stillness
Beyond the stars,
Silver of snail's way
And bone-deep scars.

Contrary element, mirror of worlds,
Where I dance
As the windy rain of November
Silvers my glance.

1970

56

Jasper

for John Jones the potter

Waxwork of a crag, a model of sea rock
In gleaming maroon –
Hear the waves break on it, see the fish fly
Under the moon!

A piece of witch-stone, jasper,
Red chalcedony
With a tidewash of grey quartz still ebbing
Back like the sea.

I was given it, it has lain in my hearth
Nearly a year
To give peace by arbitrary charm
To fingerers here.

Each hand that stroked it, gave to and took
Power out of it:
Love warmed it with whitsun, it knew
Fire-tonguing wit.

It felt stillness in half-light, it learned
Like a wild foal
To stand calm in a crowdful of noise
In its deep quartz soul.

It is Welsh rock, John. A vein of it runs
In the nape
Of the hanging coast where the oaktrees
Knot the Straits into shape.

Earth, water and fire! and a girl's hand that gave it
Dearer to me
Than gold! – I send you this shard from the wheel
Of the Welsh sea.

Your potter's eyes found glazes in red grit –
You made them yours,
The piebald debris of metallic earths,
Ragbag of ores.

We finger a pebble for luck, or chance
Magic try –
But your fingers have lived with luck so long
They must have it, or die.

And your hands chance no amateur magic:
The wheel must turn,
The wet grey clay must rise like a genie
To teapot or urn.

Yet now, because you have left Wales, and sold
Kiln and wheel
And because your cottage sinks down to its knees
In an overgrown field,

And the racks in your front-room shop
No longer fill
Quietly, quietly, with the cups and jugs
Of your fingers' skill;

And because now, though the potter's gone
And the clay dries dead,
We are glad that the love of a bride
Has graced your bed –

That ancient, amateur magic of hands,
A love and a luck
Richer than even from clay
Ever was struck –

Because of all this, on your wedding day
I send
All the power in a stone I can
To make and mend:

A piece of witch-stone, jasper,
Red chalcedony
With a tidewash of grey quartz still ebbing
Back to the sea.

1970

Life Fund

Candle End

for Di

Look, the flame grows tall.
For half an hour
This bent old crone of a wick
Will shoulder its power.

Now that you're priestess
On the tripod of art,
What is your will of it, the fire
That feeds on the heart?

Honour of a candle end
Is not piled with stones,
No mausoleum
Round your bones,

But a few moments' brightness to read by
Then light in the eyes
As the flame finally
Gutters and dies.

1971

Elegy for Brenda Chamberlain

an artist from Bangor, who took her own life, July 11, 1971

Chorus

Dead as a winkle shell
dead as a stillborn baby
dead as a bird

As a fossil is stone
as a pharaoh is stone
as a cold heart is stone

As the dust is gathered
as the dust is dry
as the dust is sterile

Dead and stone and dust
sunlight and dead and stone and dust
and dead and volcanic ash and dead

And dead.

Solo

An unhappy little person of spice and old clothes.
Delicate scrounger of kindness, being alone.
Sensitivity of an artist, ruthless and alone.

Chorus

The commodity of an illusion,
the commodity of oneself,
oneself the exploitable ore –

the veins, the raw material,
bauxite or pyrites or loadstone,
oneself the oil gusher, the deep seam of coal –

oneself the entrepreneur
of all this goodness, this refined metal,
oneself the merchant and the merchandise –

Solo

though, in her drawing, many fingers drew,
her lines not innocent of countless ages,
people of cunning, and people to watch the cunning –

Chorus

onself the capital put out at interest,
oneself the commodity of free delight,
oneself the slave in the blind night of luck ...

As the dust is gathered
as the dust is dry
as the dust is sterile –

Solo

Brenda, this death of yours,
this acquiescence in the laws of the market
– how could you do it?

O little person, how is it you never saw
that art's no art but as people take it
– this boy, that woman, this old man –

take it because it's given them,
because it's useful to them,
because it's good manners and a gift?

The giving of great art to a people
– this boy, that woman, this old man –
you'd have had no time to be dead!

W a n t e d
for JOHN and MIRIAM'S
wedding
St John's Day
1972
(being midsummer morning)

ITEM: prayer before the icon.

> We pay our respects to the saint whose festival it is,
>> the chaste one, the bare-boned and judgement-dazed
>> John, child of old age.
> His day is the opposite of Christmas. He is the
>> precurser, the elder cousin.
> He was killed to pay for the maidenhead of a girl. He
>> represents what it costs to have sex. His day
>> stands at the gateway of harvest.

ITEM: a blazing wheel, let roll from the top of a hill.

> And if it reached the bottom, that signified a good
>> crop, fair weather, and the next year off to a
>> flying start.
> They wove dry straw round the spokes of a cart-wheel.
>> In the late dusk of midsummer they set it alight,
>> and thrust it with their hands on the downward
>> path towards harvest.
> It is time to remember the rolling downhill of a wheel.
>> The year is poised in the heavens. New life is
>> the fruit we pull from the trees. The next
>> generation treads in our hearts. They pack
>> burning straw round the spokes of a tottering
>> wheel.

ITEM: blue larkspur, spikes of wild delphinium.

> Young girls were instructed to look through larkspur at
>> the bonfires of midsummer eve. This purified
>> their vision, gave protection against sore eyes.
> These flames are medicinal. But you need the petal's
>> delicacy, the innocent blue of the flower. You
>> would be well advised to look out through
>> larkspur.

ITEM: gathered on St John's Eve, seed of the fern.

> The flower is so transitory very few have seen it. On
> mid-summer eve it unfolds, golden and beautiful.
> For a few deep moments it stands entire and
> perfect. Then it crumbles quickly into dust.
> The seed of the fern was thought to be sun's blood.
> Once an archer shot an arrow into the sun's heart,
> and caught in his white handkerchief three drops
> of its blood. When he looked he saw the fern-
> seeds there.
> If you hold fern-seed in your hand it will direct you
> to all the treasures of the world. They shine
> along the ground with a violet or bluish light, as
> the fern-seed directs them.
> (And last night I cut with a flint blade, avoiding
> iron, a yellow-green frond of *Osmunda*, oldest of
> ferns. Its symmetry antedates turtles. Its arms
> cross like Pharaoh's, with the insignia of its
> office.)
> Fern-seeds contain in themselves all the light in the
> world. If you find them, they make you invisible.

ITEM: fire! fire! fire!

> On every hilltop and high place they light fires, as an
> echo or reflection of the height of the sun in
> heaven. The bonfires answer one another across
> the summits of the world.
> The day stands at the gateway of harvest. The next
> generation sings like flame at our hearts.

For the Marriage of Sara and Adrian
at Crosby, near Liverpool

(The bridegroom had been recently working as a scientist in Antarctica)

He who-looked-down-into-snow

eeee

Who-counted-the-frost
    walks with Sara in the warm way
Who-guarded-the-light
    puts his trust in darkness
Who-overcame-ice-floes
    treads softly on summer dew
Who-did-not-forget
    is loose on the streams.

eeee

Who-studied-with-honour
    strides swiftly to sunlight
the river below him
    Who-has-watched-out-the-dark
the Mersey beneath his wings
    Whose-eyes-find-knowledge
Who-brings-home-prey
    flies like a sea-eagle over the mudflats.

eeee

between Pennine and Gulf Stream
    comes he Who-reads-snow
at the estuary mouth
    Who-kisses-the-clouds
Who-homes-to-good-faith
    kneels in the groves
in the glades of his love
    Who-was-sword-in-the-wastes

eeee

Who-triumphed-in-the-ice-lands
    treads now the soft loam
Who-foraged-for-honour
    is glinting with summer dew
Who-numbered-the-winds
    is quiet with his girl
Who-stood-guard-over-fire
    walks with Sara in the twilight
the Mersey beneath his wings
    Who-homes-to-good-faith
the river beneath him
    Who-did-not-lose-heart.

        eeee

Who-mapped-out-the-clouds
    keeps his tryst in the darkness
at the estuary mouth
    Whose-eyes-find-knowledge
between mountain and sea
    Who-was-keen-in-the-wastes
like a sea-hawk over the sands
    flies he Who-keeps-faith
Who-counted-the-snow
    comes to the secret glades
Who-guarded-the-narrow-hearth
    spreads his wings on the wide sea

        eeee

Ebyevugo: for the form, see *The Heroic Recitations of the Bahima of Ankole* by
H.F. Morris (Oxford, 1964).

Lament for the 'Ship Launch'

to Howard Marshal, whistle-player

A long line is put at risk,
A world wasted of harvest,
A true tradition let slip,
An omission of music –

And for what? A woman's whim
Haughty and high-falutin
Has ruined in a short while
A fine pub and its pastime.

On Saturday at the Ship
It was a wholesome habit
For all musicians to meet
And there drink and make music.

Red Jes from his joinery there
You'd have thought a fine fiddler;
Long-haired Ian, tense with song,
On mandoline plucked plectrum.

With sly art, armed with a drum,
On bodhrán Brian Mullen
Banged the beat, heavy or light,
Of reel, hop-jig or hornpipe.

And Howard, your own slow airs
Perfected from great pipers,
Decorated with due skill
Wayward upon tin whistle ...

Now – two halves for Ma and Pa
Off flowery formica
And teenagers in lounge suits
Buy babycham and peanuts!

No more that parlour will hold
Pipers over from Ireland,
Fiddlers, professors and drunks,
Lags, labourers and students.

In every inn all you'll see
Is juke-box or tame telly,
Bleary-eyed in the beer's home
Or owlish in an alcove.

Now even the old Ship is gone,
Broken with carefree custom;
For the steel-mouthed stereo's sake
They've exiled human music.

For this pub, nothing was done,
Nobody raised the ransom -
A life betrayed, lacking care,
A long line left in danger.

1973

Deibhidhe – one of the Irish syllabic metres

Ciborium

for Jes and Sue's wedding

From a Greek word *kiborion* –
Bulbous fruit
On lotus or water-lily's
Surfacing shoot.

Canopied shrine,
A three-inch brass cup,
A goblet from a puckered stem,
Lidded on top

With a shallow-domed cupola
Gathered to a dark throat
Towering out of it, into a bud
That swells to burst out.

Some Indian villager worked it
From fire and mould,
Sweat like gold-drops on his shoulders,
Brass fiery gold.

Incised with a knife, crude patterns
Circle and flicker,
Mere hints of leafage, picked out
In green and red lacquer.

It is clearly a traditional
Shape, cut
Like thorns, like scabs of old wounds
That randomly hurt.

Ciborium, shaped like a shrine
Where the Eucharist keeps
Its white thin privacy
In the wastes of our sleep.

It came with me from where I was born –
India, the land
I'd left before I'd a tooth
Or could toddle or stand –

And what Host its emptiness holds
In the sleep of my past
I cannot reason or tell of:
Only know that at last

Such a casual token as this
Has to bear, like seeds,
The white lotus to the lake,
Lily to the reeds.

1975

An Buinnean Bui – The Yellow Bittern

for Sally when I tried to write a poem for her, three days before her wedding

Thinking of what I should give you, Sally,
Has all week
Had me imagining,
Glancing oblique

At flowers, azalea or rose,
Or fancying what risk
Might be picked in the blossom of may
That's on every hedge a mist,

And then thinking of stones –
Soft serpentine,
Black baubles of basalt,
Garnet or olivine.

Nothing has caught on my mind,
Stuck like a burr
Or made me attend to the poem
Its presence might stir.

Nothing but static in the air –
A difference
In potential between now
And three days hence.

It hangs in me like a thundercloud,
Dulls my taste,
Is anti-sex, makes thought
Go clean to waste.

I have moved through the pressure of your poem.
I am afloat
With poetry, a super-saturated solution
That a single speck or mote

Would precipitate in a crust of crystals...
But no such impurity
I can find, to settle on a single gift
A poem as surety.

No. Only the story behind a slow air
Half stirs me –
Irish, as it seems right
That for you it should be:

Of a drunk poet, one midwinter,
At the lake's edge
Finding a bird, a yellow bittern, dead
In the frozen sedge;

And thinking to himself, it must have died
Of a fearful thirst,
And swearing an oath that of all deaths
That was the worst,
But, thank God, he was unlikely himself
To die so accursed!

1976

Eros Proposes a Toast

It is customary at this sort of junketing, after the meat
    has been carved and the sauces ladled and the bones
    chewed and the puddings delicately taken with the spoon
    tipful of cream –

after the wine has been sipped and the tongues just that bit
    loosened, so that gossip can become decently improper
    between familiars and shyness divested of terror
    between those who would not, save for this feast, have
    known or cared to know of each other's existence –

it is customary, I say, for the bridegroom, answering
    obliquely the various toasts, telegrams and guffaws in
    his honour and that of his new-found wife at his side –

to stagger to his feet and himself, with as much gallantry
    as he can muster in the midst of his duplicated friends
    and quadruplicated relations, propose the bridesmaids'
    health –

that is the customary norm. And I, in common with you, my
    known allies and victims (O yes!), I, Eros the god,
    approve it, applaud and consider it good – blasé as I
    often seem on the subject of maidens – that the young
    girls who accompany the bride to the door of my
    sacrifice

should be decently thanked for their trouble and good luck
    expressed for their own journey out from their
    lack-savour virginity

towards me, the god they even now publicly worship and
    secretly, in their hearts, question and fear.

At this feast, however, bridesmaids are conspicuously
    lacking, for the good reason that we are not now met to
    lay our hopes on the moment of penetration

or to flicker a trail into this night's rumbustious lapsing
    of maidenhood or the fumbling innocence of young sap in
    my garden this maytime.

It is not that kind of nuptial. These two, look, my hands
have touched them. They have seen with my eyes, their
aloneness has heard me calling them, they have smelt my
smell in the lanes, they have tasted my salt in their
doubtings and obstinacies.

This marriage was not made today, many have witnessed it,
many have held it in affection. As a marriage it has
already gone out into the world; as a marriage it has
sown its field.

The swelling belly of the girl is no secret to you.
Fidelities have hardened within the two of them. The
procession of my spirit makes way for the coming of a
child.

Though there was no one moment of marriage or giving in
marriage, yet is this minute now the celebration of
their story. The dancers leap to answer the kicking
child in the womb.

You who are listening now, I give you the world of its
growing.

30. 4. 1977

Poems

for Lesley

Poems like moths in the air, – like granite
     Extruded down fissures,
   Like a black tree hung with snow,
   Like rain, like dark, like sunset...

As, on our marriage morning – an old man
     Pushed through the letterbox
   Four lines for fellow-feeling,
   A rooted slither of twig:

Hedd a mwyniant a dymunaf, – cariad
     Fel coron ddianaf,
   'Nawr ichwi 'Mangor Uchaf
   Y neithior hon, 'drothwy'r haf.

Or where wild garlic in gloom – between yews
     Tucks itself round gravestones,
   Shufflehome for the hedgehog,
   Slowworm's tilth, war-tent of shrews:

Where white lichen on the slate – round-tables
     Its pacific kingdom,
   Etched words of text or englyn
   Fill with the cushioning moss,

And poets have put to shame – spiders' webs,
     Cat's cradles of wordcraft:
   Like a daisy-chain of grief
   Four lines solemnise tribute.

So, each for its time and person – my poems
     Ride this strait like dinghies,
   Red sail now, and now a white,
   Close-hauled into its moment.

They gave moment to their hour – not used to
     The tradeways, the market:
   Song, epiphany or gift,
   My custom-built flotilla.

Flotilla on the fleet tide – unmoving
     Like a shoal of fishes,
    Quivering amid seaweed,
    Nosing idly the brown net.

To the trawl-net of this book – and the price
     Outrageous as ever! –
    They tread water, bewildered,
    Are commodity at last.

Last night, at birth or wedding – funeral,
     Visit of friend or bard,
    They honoured a remembrance,
    Celebration, feast or dream.

Now, in the dream-bare morning – on the quay
     The eyes of honour glaze.
    In boxes slithery with ice
    Is end of time and person.

             1977

Blodeuwedd and other poems

Elegy for the Welsh Dead,
in the Falkland Islands, 1982

Gwyr a aeth Gatraeth oedd ffraeth eu llu.
Glasfedd eu hancwyn, a gwenwyn fu.
         – *Y Gododdin* (6th century)

(Men went to Catraeth, keen was their company.
They were fed on fresh mead, and it proved poison.)

Men went to Catraeth. The luxury liner
For three weeks feasted them.
They remembered easy ovations,
Our boys, splendid in courage.
For three weeks the albatross roads,
Passwords of dolphin and petrel,
Practised their obedience.
Where the killer whales gathered,
Where the monotonous seas yelped.
Though they went to church with their standards
Raw death has them garnished.

Men went to Catraeth. The Malvinas
Of their destiny greeted them strangely.
Instead of affection there was coldness,
Splintering iron and the icy sea,
Mud and the wind's malevolent satire.
They stood nonplussed in the bomb's indictment.

Malcolm Wigley of Connah's Quay. Did his helm
Ride high in the war-line?
Did he drink enough mead for that journey?
The desolated shores of Tegeingl,
Did they pig this steel that destroyed him?
The Dee runs silent beside empty foundries.
The way of the wind and the rain is adamant.

Clifford Elley of Pontypridd. Doubtless he feasted.
He went to Catraeth with a bold heart.
He was used to valleys. The shadow held him.
The staff and the fasces of tribunes betrayed him.
With the oil of our virtue we have annointed
His head, in the presence of foes.

Phillip Sweet of Cwmbach. Was he shy before girls?
He exposes himself now to the hags, the glance
Of the loose-fleshed whores, the deaths
That congregate like gulls on garbage.
His sword flashed in the wastes of nightmare.

Russell Carlisle of Rhuthun. Men of the North
Mourn Rheged's son in the castellated vale.
His nodding charger neighed for the battle.
Uplifted hooves pawed at the lightning.
Now he lies down. Under the air he is dead.

Men went to Catraeth. Of the forty-three
Certainly Tony Jones of Carmarthen was brave.
What did it matter, steel in the heart?
Shrapnel is faithful now. His shroud is frost.

With the dawn men went. Those forty-three,
Gentlemen all, from the streets and byways of Wales,
Dragons of Aberdare, Denbigh and Neath –
Figment of empire, whore's honour, held them.
Forty-three at Catraeth died for our dregs.

Potatoes

for Brace, a civil servant

Potato haulms grasp at the rain.
Gnarled hands
Like earthen dwarf hands, like gross
Seaweed fronds

Clutch at our low sky. Western promise
In the soil
Is waiting for glut. Rounding tubers
Await our toil.

Market forces dictate, not hunger.
To hold the price
We dye wide acres of them blue, leave them
For eelworm or mice.

At the other end of the world
The Sahara
Dusts out the grasslands.
The weary farmer

Starves in the ash of his crop.
Great bones
Of high-shouldered cattle whiten
Like standing stones.

And for us, wheat burns, crops
Are dug in,
Coffee beans thrown in the sea.
The financier's spin

Of the dice, the market, dictates.
Our charity, even,
Puts money in our purse.
Thatcher or Reagan

Give our kindness its voice.
But you, Brace,
Civil servant, bureaucrat,
The Janus face

Looking both ways to two worlds,
Serving the market
Yet knowing that in the wages you earn
Lurk plan and target –

In that mindful view of things that you
As bureaucrat
Know as the perfection proper to you,
Greed and waste like that

Should be impossible. Capitalists
May dump their goods,
Sink coffee or burn wheat; but good bureaucrats
Don't poison spuds.

1985

A Square of Grey Slate

presented to Pedro Perez Sarduy, Cuban poet, at the
Wales-Cuba Resource Centre at the National Eisteddfod
1985 in Rhyl

Days I have been wondering, Señor,
How I should speak:
The very language I use being wrong
For Eisteddfod week,

And yet I'm not satisfied
To mumble it glumly
As a mere *lingua franca*
Between Cuba and Cymru.

My tongue's my own, True Thomas says.
How then
Can I speak in the crowding name of all Welsh
Women and men

To offer you, Señor, the brotherhood
Of Welsh Wales?
How can I strike red fire from the very iron
Of our chains?

This morning early, I went to my rainy garden
Hoping to find
A messenger – perhaps a riddle
Of times out of mind –

A palimpsest of my people, a forgotten tryst
That I could keep
For them this Monday morning
Of Eisteddfod week.

There in the path was this square of grey slate.
Let that stone
Be my herald, I said, let its mute cry down the years
Atone

For my English. Let it speak
Where I cannot
Of the Welshness of Wales
Now, on this spot.

Men die here for stone. The ancient strata eroded
By rain, by frost,
Till the massif's a mere negative
Of what it was...

Señor, stone is the stuff of oppression
In this land.
Look, the conqueror's castles, Rhyddlan, Rhuthun, Denbigh
Still stand.

No one in Wales is untouched by rock.
Coal and slate
– Laid down before dinosaurs walked the world –
Dominate

Vast tracts of our industry, our past.
It was for stone
That the shanty-towns mushroomed
To chapel and home.

Rock was our vortex. Our working class
Was drilled from it.
Their dream and their discipline answered
The greed of the rich.

Strike. Lock-out. Depression.
Let this stone lip
Tell of those terrible years.
Now, slate-tip, coal-tip

Rear up like pyramids. Pharaoh and Israelite
Share
The memorial of the dump
Under wide air.

Welsh poets in love, Llywelyn Goch, Dafydd or Iolo,
Used to sing
Poems to thrush or tomtit, salmon or north wind
– Anything

Under the moon that moved, he'd make it
Ambassador,
Messenger, *llatai* for him, to travel
Straight to his girl's door

And tell her how much he loved her
And how much
He died, died for the sight of her,
Died for her touch.

Now therefore I command this square of grey slate
To go *llatai* for me
Through Westerlies and Trades
To the Carib Sea.

Go, little Fidelista of slate,
To the midmost
Of the Americas, where the plumes of royal palm
Mark Cuba's coast.

Go to the sugarcane fields, the rice paddies,
The orchards –
Go where the blacks once died like flies
As the cash flowed northwards.

And tell them, slateling, about our country,
This place of stone
At the edge of Capital's shadow
As the day comes on.

Gooseberries

for Mike Donahue, killed in
a car crash August 1985

They sat in my bowl, globular, tawny
And so ripe
They wanted to burst. My fingers
Had burns in the grip.

When you pick them, prickles seem friendly
Like the kneading pins
Of a kitten in your lap. The bushes walk home to be milked.
Their udders swing

In the sun-tanned lanes. They demand that you
Pick them, pick them,
Every last berry that has bent
Shoot and stem

To the waiting earth. From the pricketty bush
All Saturday
My thumbs pulled gold. In punnets and bowls
Green gallons lay.

And that night I walked to the pub
Whimsical
From the gooseberries' rock 'n roll
Festival.

'Mike, if you like gooseberries,' I said,
'You can have a ton
For the taking.' 'Ah, they're lovely,' you said, 'grapes
With whiskers on!'

'They're over-ripe, bursting,' I said, 'but the flavour's
Too good to waste.'
I watched your imagination bend to them
Savouring the taste.

'A bit of fermentation never did anyone
Much harm.
We'll come for them.' A gooseberry tryst wafted
On the breath of barm

Bubbled quietly into your sleep. You had drunk
Well and happily
At someone's do. Promises could keep.
Time had the key...

But earth waits for fruit. That Sunday night,
Screams and tearing
Of brakes, hurtling of steel in the rain,
And an end of caring.

I remember the hospitality of your presence,
How we came into it
As if we were lost in the cold, to a hearth where a wood fire
Has long been lit.

How you drew your world round you, layer on layer,
Round a fire
That you feared was anarchic at heart – could break out
Brutal and dire

With an open madness of suffering, to shame you
And leave you
Apprehensive of friends whose shocked kindness
Had tried to ease you.

Well, well. Gooseberries, like Irish harps,
Sing the sweeter
The closer they are to bursting.
World was completer

(So it seemed, Mike) for you then:
Marriage and job
And family, all rounded in some manner of peace.
The berries bobbed

On the leaning twigs, the songs were tawny with power,
The love could open.
I remember a friend, a singer, a lover of gooseberries
Gathered and broken.

Pardon me, therefore, if I keep this gooseberry tryst
Too late.
The fruit returns to the earth. Mike Donahue,
Peace to your fate.

A Milk Toast

for Jean Gregson, newborn

Milks are distinguishable.
Our own wild kind
I've not tasted since times
Out of mind.

You've to work for it now,
Tugging to feed
At a gorged nipple
Playful with need.

For you – for most of us – soon
Milk will mean
Packaging, bottles or cartons
Sealed by machine –

Cow juice or dairy product,
Something to cloud
Black coffee or tea
To a palatable brown.

I am old enough
To have gone out
In a sweet-pea sort of morning
To a horse and cart,

A blue-striped jug in my hands
To be ladled full
From a churn with sliding whiteness
Not quite cool.

I pour a glass, remembering. Bubbles
Coagulate
For a second, then thin
Wretchedly, and break.

But this, too, is milk – sterilized
Friesian stuff,
A *lingua franca* of dairies,
Minimal enough!

Oh, a lot talk of blood. Blue blood,
Sine qua non
Of lordly thugs. Hot blood
Of the torrid zone.

Flesh and blood. A matter of lacking
A proper cell wall
And therefore part of the minority kingdom,
An animal.

But we, from common crawlers, distinguish
Our mammary past.
In the night of the Saurian day, milk not blood
Gave us class.

Sucking is our definitive labour.
Lips and hands –
Both of them work to ensure that supply
Matches demand.

Suckle and suck: milk's reciprocity
Is primal.
Love shall always have lips for us now.
So long as we're mammal

Food shall be common ground,
Represent
For us potential of Agape,
Missa, what is sent.

The love-feast re-enacts lactation.
Communion
Or Christmas Dinner, both half-remember
That topless union.

Suckle and suck. Communicants
Of heart and lip –
Their proto-speech gathers as milk
Surges and dips.

(And indeed our labial stops,
Fricatives,
Liquids and aspirate gasps
Are sucking's negative,

Pulled out instead of in, as speech
Gives new contexts
To the pillow-talk
Of mouth and breast.)

Birds warble from their throats. Crickets
Rasp wings.
A man learns the truth from our lips.
We are milk things,

And therefore, Jean,
For your birthday
I raise this glass to you.
May milk-light stay

For you always as sanity. May relationships
Be built
At lip level. Be worthy, not of red blood,
But of milk.

                              1985

A Fern from Skye

for Somhairle MacGill-eain
(Sorley Maclean)

'Lament for the Children'
– a pibroch by Padraig Mór MacCruimein

1

We came across two worlds to see you, Sorley,
To Skye
The last battlefield, the last
Never say die

Of the Gael: the Celtic world squeezed out,
Cauterized for sheep;
Its leaders angled in sharp practice;
Highland and creek

Emptied of the tribes;
Croft and song
Left rotting like bladderwrack
On the high strand.

2

It was here, in Peinnachorrain of the Braes,
That the tenants held fast,
Met and showed fight. Broken head,
Clout and gasp

By their intransigence, refused
That grey day
At the sea coast, to be dumped
Or carted away.

Visitors we came. Clean air delighted us, gull music,
Cottages
Under the hill, clinking of little streams
And a damp breeze

From Raasay across the Sound. But you, you live here,
Poet, among
The presentative past of your people.
The old tongue

You teach to seed, in the imagination's
Freehold
To grow and in untoward time, to green bare rock
Like veins of gold.

3

To a tryst I'd come. For fifteen years
I'd fingered the coin
Of our one meeting together, kept our currency
Of talk warm

In the pockets of my heart.
Poet –
Greatest in these islands now – here's that groat for you,
Look, my hand holds it!

4

But your cottage was closed. You were away!
In the filtering light
Tangled woods and wet places
Of Raasay were bright...

But as I turned to join my children already
Racing down
In the joyous concentration of shingle and sand,
The shrill sound

Of them dimmed in the great space like oystercatchers',
Like peewits',
And their mother walking between them, drawing them after her
For all their tricks

Like a shepherd to the best pasture –
As I turned,
It was your wall caught my eye: the piled stones, stonecrop
And the mats of fern.

5

Male fern, was it? Branching stocks,
Stiff straight frond
Crinked and each pinna upturned to the air – no,
It felt wrong! –

Dryopteris oreades then? Pioneer
Of high screes,
Not under a thousand feet, the books say,
Nor by the sea.

A highland plant, its distribution
Not fully known –
Not, certainly, expected in the sea-level
Stones of your home.

For a moment it seems like the Gael himself –
Its history
A lost unexpectedness, a perfecting
Entelechy

Informing the blue distances.
Not for it
The plush leafmould of a wood.
Rock its roots fit.

6

Rock. And a great music.
Apprehension
Of the fern resonating
To the taut scansion

Of that ground. Piper pulls the lament
Round him,
Walks the contemplative ways
The air has found him.

Slow measure of this music's
Magnanimity.
A reaching certainty. Sorrow
Between cloud and sea.

Each variation affects the light,
Each singling
Of gracenotes the geometry of this
Lament for the children.

For the children who are not.
For those died
In all ages, now. For those
In the hunger have died.

For the Gael who loses this music.
For the children.
For me, O Conaráin of the Curraigh,
This grace singling.

7

Oreades in the stone. Music's geometry
Along your wall
Makes interface. People with real names
Find your door.

The heart has freehold. Green veins
Of a poetry
Gold in the rock. Black roots
Between cloud and sea.

The children circle the beach. Their antennae
Gather
Treasure from the stones – a shell,
A curlew's feather...

I thought, you wouldn't mind. I widged
With my knife
A tiny crown – this fern – from the mat
Of its crinkled life.

It grows now by my kitchen window.
My daughters carp
As they come from school, their Welsh words
Tugged and sharp

And flown across its space like a kite
In the wind.
It uncurls in its own time still.
It chooses to sing.

1985

New Poems

Il Dolce Stil

Bill Tydeman, who once taught a course on Courtly
Love with me, also lost his mother that 14th February, 1988

On the far barbican used to be a garden
Where snowdrop and primrose showed at this season.
Under the naked thorn, frost fingers harden.

A voice cries, 'You who taught love, you and another,
Now in the coincidence of Love's reason
Valentine's morning grieves both for a mother.'

1988

The Harp and the Stag

An Irish punt *coin for Margaret and Dug's wedding*
when they were going to live in Dublin

The rapid gracenotes like wit
Round the room etch a music
Not there these two hundred years
Since want humbled the harpers.

The secret's lost, learnt so well,
And the silver strings broken:
Already Bunting was blind
To blind Hempson's playing.

Though even then, when those long nails
Rested, and the rich silence
Moulded a momentary ground
That might once have been Ireland,

Even then, no other would play.
They'd not gainsay that glory
And the old harper stumped home,
Unchallenged and unbeaten.

★

I have heard high music play –
Clancy in Miltown Malbay,
Keening and cry in a piece
Fingered by Séamus Ennis.

Hornpipe, polka and reel
At Quilty on the whistle
Of a lame man's dancing breath.
Michaeleen at the Roadside.

All the great ones, but this, this
That echoes round the stasis
Of the heart hundreds of years
Since the hurt to the harpers ...

No, never again! One side –
Eire, and the coin dated,
The Trinity harp etched out,
The silence that surrounds it.

★

But turn over, the great stag,
Seven-tined, bells its challenge
Where the waste and mangled wit
Erodes like the Atlantic.

The other side of the coin,
The green hills of Leinster,
The hart that walks Stephen's Green
And Dublin's disillusion;

Or where the waterfalls flow
In the west winds of Sligo,
And the long stacks of cut peat
The boglands disinherit;

Or in Dingle, by Slea Head,
Its delicate hoof tempted
To the beehive huts for grass
Greener than bare hillside –

With horned Cernunos, a beast
Of purpose in the breeding –
Ancient of the world, my stag
Of Ireland bells its challenge.

1994

Angelological

i.m. Peter Hoy, Fellow of Merton

Bangor, dear city of angels! –
The sad anguish it has gone
Like thought, like a secret thought
In the ebbtide of morning.

We were young angels then. Books
Would be written, were present,
Were already in the world –
Angelological journals,
Cherubic notebooks, Poems
Englished from the Seraphim:
Principalities and Powers
Attended on our book launch.

An angel is where it thinks.
It has no need of recall.
Gabriel wants no memory
To kneel in annunciation.
The Last Trump is at his lips.
Lucifer, the morning Star,
Cannot choose but be falling,
Falling, falling, for the fall
Contaminates his thinking
– Where he is – to the extent
Of time, duration of place.

An angel is where it thinks.
Infinity of cherubs
Laugh at the same joke, lament
Over one sparrow's mishap.
Seraphim with sleepless eye
Veil their God-ravished faces
With the long wings' flight-feathers.
They have watched out the big bang.
They see beyond the light years
To the exploding Nothing.
Their art clears the primal soup,
The opaqueness of creation.

Peter, it was only last week
I finished one intention:
The Angelogical Notebook
Lay flush in the printing tray.
DOS and format and WordStar
Had revealed and done their worst.
This was your book. To no one
Else, mon confrère, dear angel,
Would it be dedicated
In the public domain of print.

And then the phone. You were dead.
The crying perturbation
Of what to do with a life
Ransacked from so much learning
Faltered in the receiver.
No angel can claim such grief.
Already you were fading
Out of reach of your thought.
Problematic where you were –
Moulted, tail and flight-feathers.
Did you kneel? Were there trumpets
Tongued flashingly in the wind?
Now you can never be sent
Angelological journals,
Fading, and merely human
Not where your thought is – dead, dead,
In the wisp of a white body
That the savage heart has torn.

1994

Knots

for Abigail

Sailors, astride a yard,
Knotted the square sails
When storms blew hard.

Reefed to half, the bleached
Canvas did not capsize.
Harbour was reached.

Under and over, the ties
Hanging from the loud
Sail's clap-belly, udder-wise,

Must be reached for and tied
Over and under. And if
Frozen fingers plied

Under and under instead,
The reef would slide,
The ship be buffeted

To Davy Jones. Lacing your shoe
You've tied a granny.
Such bows undo.

Badly or well
You can knot sail or boot,
So with a birthday spell:

Let the true yarn be told –
In the salty typhoon
Hunched canvas hold!

Or, changing metaphor,
May no dangling granny
Trip to the floor!

1995

106

Ruth at Taizé

Sadnesses walk tiptoe across the clearing,
Like old age they don't come single.
Parting of companions,
Childhood regrets –

Group themselves like a corps de ballet
Round fantasy or grief.
Persecution, hard duty, loss
Are mirrors for them.

The choreography's too easy –
Yourself as tragic heroine,
Sadnesses a-quiver on their points,
The dead prince of Meaning.

No, in a sacred place, where the reality of pilgrims
Opens to the sun,
Be challenged, Ruth – you and the sadnesses.
A true tale awaits you.

How you must find simple well-water
At the world's end.
Help fish, hare, old crone.
How you must ask.

But to bring water back
Across those continents of Now? –
Fingers won't hold it, it escapes
To the worm and seed.

With empty hands still wet
You can lead the sadnesses
Into a King's bedchamber.
The dead prince lives your touch.

Worm in its crevice turns.
Seed through its sleep of eighteen years
Pushes green leaf.
Is it you that wake?

1996

Acknowledgements

These poems have been taken from the following collections:

Formal Poems (Christopher Davies, 1960), *Asymptotes* (privately printed, 1963), *Poems 1951-67* (Deiniol Press and Gee & Son, 1974), *Spirit Level* (Christopher Davies, 1974), *Life Fund* (Gomer, 1979), *Blodeuwedd and other poems* (Poetry Wales Press, 1988). Many of them were also privately printed for their appropriate occasions.

Some poems have appeared in the following magazines:

Dock Leaves, Anglo-Welsh Review, The Dublin Magazine, Stand, Planet, Poetry Wales, Mabon, Y Dyfodol, Omnibus, Cuba Si (The Magazine of the Britain-Cuba Resource Centre), *The Future of the Word* (the first WUW Register), *Chanter* (the magazine of the Bagpipe Society)

and in the following anthologies:

Poems '71 ed. Jeremy Hooker (Gomer), *Poems '72* ed. John Ackerman (Gomer), *Poems '76* ed. Glyn Jones (Gomer), *Anthology of Contemporary Poetry* ed. John Wain (Hutchinson, 1979), *Anglo-Welsh Poetry 1480-1980* ed. Raymond Garlick & Roland Mathias (Poetry Wales Press), *Wales in Verse* ed. Dannie Abse (Secker & Warburg, 1983), *Discovering Welshness* ed. Oliver Davies & Fiona Bowie (Gomer 1992) and *Burning the Bracken* ed. Amy Wack (Seren, 1996).